Guide to

PIMLICO

By James Dowsing

SUNRISE PRESS

34 CHURTON ST, LONDON

Why Pimlico?

Opinion differs as to the origin of the name but during Tudor times a worthy publican, one Ben Pimlico, apparently kept an inn at Hoxton. His beer, of a fine "nut browne", acquired fame throughout London, and there is still a Pimlico Walk in Hoxton. It appears the name was copied by a pub near the present Victoria Station where Pimlico was recorded by 1626.

The western portion of the area was called the **Neat Houses**, after the mediaeval manor of Neat House. This was situated on the present Abbots Manor housing estate; until the Reformation it belonged to Westminster Abbey. Neat is derived from Neyte, meaning islet–a particularly appropriate title since the farmhouse occupied a piece of high ground amid tidal inlets. In time, as some semi-rural housing began the vicinity became known as Neathouses.

During last century the area of Pimlico was often referred to as **South Belgravia**. The name was not unjustified, especially for the north western corner of Pimlico. Again, Belgravia and Pimlico, along with Mayfair, originally made up the Grosvenor Estate, and were developed at about the same time.

COVER: Corner house in Gloucester Street

PAGE ONE: St. Saviour's spire, Moreton Place

Pimlico is a slightly dreamy island in a bend of the Thames . . . and, architecturally, as much as wonderland today as it was for Londoners of 140 years ago. It was in the forefront of the capital's great property developments; it was the largest ever undertaken by one builder, that man being Thomas Cubitt.

Out of the marshland rose street after street of terraced houses, thousand on thousand of them, and the whole marked with a classical unity—an unfailing style, a purpose—that mirrored its close relation, Belgravia. Pimlico was not called "Stuccoville" for nothing. Today its elegance is tinged with nostalgia and charm that will delight the visitor if he takes time to explore and savour.

ART DECO found expression in the area in the form of the New Victoria cinema, now the Apollo Victoria theatre. Built in 1929, at the height of a slightly crazed motion picture boom, the exterior did not match the Firestone or Hoover buildings elsewhere in London, but once inside the filmgoer was treated to a fairy palace of the sea. The architect was William Trent, who collaborated with E. Walmsley Lewis for the interior. Shell-like fittings abound with the intention of creating an exotic, underwater cavern effect. What had that to do with the "flicks"? A premonition of Esther Williams perhaps, who was yet a schoolgirl? Never mind, it is a fine example of the super cinema of the period.

AUBREY BEARDSLEY. At Number 114 **Cambridge Street** lived an artist who promised so much, particularly in book illustration, yet died at the age of 25. He won fame, and notoriety, in his brief life; his designs for Oscar Wilde's "Salome" shocked the time. It has not prevented Beardsley from being recognised as a major influence in English graphic art and true son of the aesthetic movement of the 1890's. He spent two years at Number 114, with his mother and sister, before worsening tuberculosis sent him to warmer shores. He died in France in 1898 and is among the foremost of the many "artistic folk"—music teachers, writers and painters—who lived in Pimlico last century.

B

BESSBOROUGH GARDENS represents one of the focal points in London of the Crown Estates and their rebuilding works are much in evidence. Who would imagine that a spired gothic church—Holy Trinity, by name—once filled part of the square? A fine companion to St.Saviour's and St.Gabriel's, it fell to the wrecker's blow, along with the Rank-Hovis building beside Vauxhall Bridge. Until 1980 porticoed terraces faced three sides of the square; these were replaced in a similar style and the effect is pleasing. Behind them, in **Bessborough Street**, is a charming little gatehouse which was built as part of the redevelopment. Across the road are some 20th century designs, including the many-sided brick office structure which seems decidedly overbearing. A plaque near the entrance notes the Crown Estates connection and lists architect and builder, in this case the ever-present Harry Neal.

BIOGRAPH CINEMA, formerly in Wilton Road, opened in 1905 and was a pioneer in film exhibition in Britain. Initially called the Bioscope the interior structure remained unchanged. A plaque in the foyer claimed the title of England's first cinema. Bioscope, it said, was the original name for film houses and "in fact are still called Bioscope in South Africa". In 1896 a building was erected at Olympia, London, to house "Theatregraph", promoted by Robert Paul. The Biograph's undeniable feat of almost 80 years of screening, not at an exhibitions centre but beside a major rail terminal, must command the respect of any film buff. It was demolished in 1983.

BLEWCOAT SCHOOL. Through a forest of modern buildings near Victoria Street one comes upon a 17th century dollshouse where once the poor children of the area received a rudimentary education. Now National Trust property, a statue of a blue-clad lad still stands, in the practice of the time, above the doorway, as does the clock which no doubt turned too slowly for the pupils. The building, in **Caxton Street**, is a tribute to the good, red-brick sense of that era.

THE BLITZ. Because of its nearness to the Southern Railway terminus Pimlico could not escape its share of German bombs. The occasional gaps in continuity in many terraces are witness to the devastation. During raids many residents took shelter at St. James tube station and in trenches dug in Vincent Square. One of the worst horrors occurred in **Sutherland Street** when an entire terrace was demolished, killing 20 people and injuring 55. One man was blown a quarter of a mile and lived. The nearby Monster pub, long a landmark in Pimlico, was destroyed.

A month later, on 11th May, 1941, a bomb passed through Turner Buildings on the Millbank Estate, destroying one side of the block of flats. Twenty-four people died; another twenty, trapped in surface shelters, were brought out after 1½ hours of digging by rescue crews.

BRIDEWELL PRISON. In the vicinity of Army & Navy Stores and Westminster Cathedral prisoners once paraded and cursed their fate. This was the site of

Entrance to Moreton Mews . . . cheddar cheese a speciality

Westminster Bridewell, built in 1655 to house the lawbreakers of St. Margaret's parish. Nearby was **Greencoat School**, dedicated in 1633 to shelter orphans. The institution was known earlier as St. Margaret's Hospital and both names linger in street signs in the vicinity.

BURDETT-COUTTS SCHOOL recalls the fact that the area had another notable benefactor last century in addition to George Peabody. Angela Burdett-Coutts, grand-daughter of the banker Thomas Coutts, was created baroness by Queen Victoria in recognition of her generosity to London and its people. The primary school in **Rochester Street** was but one project. It was accompanied by the building of St. Stephen's Church, Rochester Row, whose broad admirable interior would do honour to a large provincial centre.

Baroness Burdett-Coutts succeeded to her fortune at an early age, and during her life financed all manner of charitable schemes, ranging from the setting up of a new central market for London, which failed but brought improvements elsewhere, to paying the passages of Irish people to Canada. Sadly St. Stephen's, her Westminster memorial, was long deprived of the top of its spire because of crumbling stonework. The Church lacked the funds to undertake the repair. In 1994, however, a fibre-glass replacement was lowered onto the stump of the old steeple.

C

CAMBRIDGE STREET. If Pimlico is seen as a smallish town, somewhat bypassed, surely this thoroughfare must represent its high street, rather than Warwick Way. Let the visitor go to the upper end, look southward—then disagree with this romantic contention. To the right the neat, no-nonsense Clarendon public house lords over a clutch of small shopfronts; the terrace houses converge in the distance, quiet, unhurried; and completing the provincial scene soars the tower and spire of St. Gabriel's. Surely, one thinks, the church has stood guard since mediaeval times. The records say no; a mere 120 years or more.

CHELSEA BRIDGE, in a suspension form, is one of the most attractive over the Thames. The present structure was opened in 1937 following rebuilding of the original 1858 bridge. The earlier crossing had the distinction of being opened by the Prince of Wales, later Edward VII. It collected a toll, a fact so resented that charges were dropped 20 years later.

CHESHIRE VILLAGES would not seem to have much in common with the urban spread of Pimlico. Not so. Belgrave Road, Waverton Street, Eccleston Square and Claverton and Churton Streets were named after villages in that county. It is not coincidental since the original Grosvenor estates were located in Chester and vicinity.

CHURCHILL GARDENS were begun in 1946 and the estate now means home and village to 5,500 people. It has its own primary school and pubs, with Lupus Street acting as the "high street". The project, designed by Powell & Moya and rising above a mere 33 acres, is best viewed from the Thames railway bridge; the sight is not unimpressive.

D

DEPARTMENT OF ENVIRONMENT. At one end of Pimlico looms Battersea Power Station (begun 1929), and at the other the triple slabs of this government body, built in the Sixties. Side by side like grey waffles popping from a toaster the offices, in **Marsham Street**, house a legion of civil servants, including the suite of the minister. What a shame that a department charged with improving our surroundings should have such grubby ramparts where it backs onto Monck Street. And why so much concrete, rather than greenery, about the entrances? The towers are not without beauty from a distance, and the visitor should not miss the 17th century street sign set into the corner with **Great Peter Street**.

DENBIGH STREET, like so many others in the district, was named for its general aristocratic sound, rather than any specific connection, when all the Grosvenor family names had been exhausted. Present-day residents may be surprised to know that one 19th century journalist, writing in 1877, found their street "prissy" yet tranquil. Nevertheless in the 1980's the architectural style of lower Denbigh Street does retain a distinct fastidiousness.

DOLPHIN SQUARE. If Pimlico represents an early 19th century instance of improved town living Dolphin Square (1937; architect, Gordon Jeeves) must epitomise the pre-war dream of much the same thing — using only a tiny proportion of the original Pimlico area. Which is the better: the cool, columned streets of Cubitt or Jeeves's stacked, red-brick apartments? The square covers 7½ acres and comprises 1,200 flats. Previously the area had been occupied by Cubitt's yard and the army clothing depot.

EBURY BRIDGE AND SQUARE recall the manor of the same name which stood nearby. Its lands comprised a wide area, including most of Pimlico. In mediaeval times it was owned by the church. The Reformation changed all that, and eventually it passed to Hugh Audley (1577-1662), who had accumulated estates throughout the county. He outlived his direct heirs and Ebury went in time to the guardians of

Mary Davies. At the age of seven a marriage was proposed, for the sum of £5,000, with the Berkeley heir, but the money was not forthcoming. Instead Mary, at 12, was wed to Sir Thomas Grosvenor, of a Chester family of baronets.

Today, the square is dominated by flats and offices, yet here, centuries ago, it is far from unlikely that the sovereigns of England, out for the hunt, passed by with the hounds, or stopped to quench a thirst. The name Ebury has been described as of Saxon origin: Ey, signifying water, and burgh, fortified place. In 1307 Edward I was recorded as giving permission for the manor's fortification.

ECCLESTON SQUARE. Apart from Downing Street how many London streets can say, "Winston Churchill lived here"? Pimlico can make this claim. For four years (1909-1913) the Churchills resided at Number 33, at a time when he was very much an up-and-coming man in British politics. While at Eccleston Square he was, in rapid succession, President of the Board of Trade, Home Secretary (1910), and then First Lord of the Admiralty (1911). He was in his thirties. The family vacated the house shortly before the outbreak of war, and the immediate years were to bring the taste of failure over the Dardenelles campaign, and his dropping from Cabinet.

The square takes its name from a village in the Grosvenor's home county of Cheshire. The terraces were begun in 1835 making it the earliest of the Pimlico residential gardens. The date is reflected in the uneven character of the houses— some higher, some lower, a number sharing extended porticoes—as if the developer was feeling his way. The square's nearness to Belgravia always made it worthy of attention, yet in its own right it has a breadth and dignity not too often found in a modern city.

FOCH STATUE. Marshal Ferdinand Foch (1851-1929), generalissimo of the victorious forces in World War I, is honoured by an equestrian statue in **Grosvenor Gardens**. Fittingly, surrounding buildings are fashioned in a distinct French manner. Marshal Foch commanded forces at Ypres (1914), during the offensive of Vimy Ridge (1915) and led French armies on the British right in the battle of the Somme in 1916. With other generals he fell from favour briefly as the Western Front stalemate dragged on, but in May 1917 was appointed chief of staff. Later he became supremo, at least in name, of the French and British armies, and of the Americans and Belgians. On two important occasions he substantially overturned the views of the British commander-in-chief Haig. During 1918 he pursued the war to a successful, if weary and sorrowful, conclusion. He is buried near Napoleon in the Invalides.

The lower end of Tachbrook Street

G

GARDENERS, HIGHWAYMEN AND OTHERS. The Times, when noting the spread of housing south of Belgravia, reminded readers that these fields provided London markets with some of their earliest and best vegetables. The gardeners tilled their plots as tenants of the Grosvenor board, with little or no security of tenure. When the builders moved in delaying tactics were adopted, such as the planting of licorice, which is difficult to eradicate; some refused to budge. One grower held out for three years, while another whose family had been in the vicinity over a long period, was found an alternative patch. But their cause was hopeless before the growth of the metropolis.

The arrival of Johnson, Cubitt and other developers put an end to the comparative isolation which had attracted highwaymen, plain thieves and cutthroats from earliest times. It was a refuge within convenient distance of the West End. One would-be Dick Turpin is said to have had a cottage in the area of what is today **Warwick Square.**

GRAND BOULEVARDS. As straight as two matching arrows, **St. George's Drive** and **Belgrave Road** dissect residential Pimlico, to be joined at their southern ends by the equally noble **Lupus Street.** The dimensions of the three were generous for the time, with the latter being crowned by the vista of St. Saviour's. Despite the parade of vehicles from Victoria Coach Station, St. George's Drive, in its quieter moments, is perhaps the most impressive—its grandeur heightened by the sight of the tower and spire of St. Michael's, Chester Square, another creation of Thomas Cundy (1846).

GREYCOAT HOSPITAL. The area once was alive with grey, blue and green apparel, each colour denoting a different institution for poor children. A Greycoat School for boys was opened in 1698 in the Broad Sanctuary, Westminster, partly to combat juvenile begging and to impart Christian beliefs. In 1701 it moved to **Greycoat Place** and became a boarding school for boys and girls. During Queen Anne's reign it was designated a Royal Foundation (1706) and served the congested, often badly housed area for 150 years. In 1874 the boys departed, and the school catered solely for girls, some 300 in all. The building was restored after bomb damage during World War II. Today it has 450 pupils, with a similar number in lower grades at its Sloane Square branch.

GROSVENOR CANAL, built in 1823, still cascades through sluice-gates near Chelsea Bridge. It played a major role in the development of housing in the area. The canal lead from Grosvenor Basin, situated where Victoria Station now stands, down to the Thames, and made it possible for building materials and infill soil to be brought with comparative ease into the heart of the district. The Grosvenor board charged 4d. a ton on cargoes. though shipments of soil were exempt, and in 1842 it collected £1,437. Many firms, including builders, had premises on the rim of the basin in what is today **Buckingham Palace Road.**

GROSVENOR ROAD, the main road skirting the Thames, is the only thoroughfare in Pimlico to carry the Duke of Westminster's family name. For much of its course it is accompanied by the embankment, some of which was built at Cubitt's expense.

Paradise Road

A quarter century after the building of Pimlico the area was able to win a very good press in a newspaper article, titled "Stuccoville", published in 1877:
"Here are squares and churches. South Belgravia is genteel, sacred to professional men of various grades, not rich enough to luxuriate in Belgravia, but rich enough to live in private houses—for this is a retired suburb. Here people are more lively than in Kensington, though not so grand, of course as Albertopolis, and yet a cut above Chelsea, which is only commercial, and ever so much more respectable than Westminster, dreadfully behind the age, vegetating the other side of Vauxhall Bridge Road."

The writer went on to name specific streets, away from the grander squares, which were particularly well regarded. "The genteel part lies in a small space in the immediate neighbourhood of **Gloucester**, **Sussex**, **Cambridge** and **Sutherland** Streets, while **Lupus Street** is the sweet south that borders this paradise of rest. This is the abode of gentility—a servant or two in the kitchen, birds in the windows, with flowers in boxes, pianos, and the latest fashions of course. People here are always dressed in their best, and though not cream of the cream, can show on occasion broughams and pairs; opera cloaks of surpassing gorgeousness and dress suits that would satisfy Poole or Worth. Where people do not live on their property they are artists—they teach the piano, singing, dancing, drawing, languages, or are in the City."

The newspaper article described **Westmoreland Street** as "quakerish", while **Warwick Way** had adopted barrow selling of hosiery and vegetables in a thoroughly successful manner.

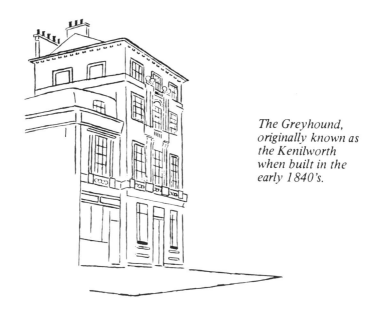

The Greyhound, originally known as the Kenilworth when built in the early 1840's.

Cubitt had to contend with a scattering of business firms which had set up on the waterside over many years and which, not unnaturally, were opposed to his scheme. The name Grosvenor stems from the French "Gros Veneur", great hunter. It was the name of William the Conqueror's nephew, from whom the family claim descent.

H

HOLY APOSTLES CHURCH. Who would know it today?–but in **Claverton Street** once stood a mighty Wesleyan church with five columns outside and grand, curving gallery within. It passed to the Catholic community until its devastation in the Blitz. Services continued in accommodation provided by the Church of England, a fine example of the Christian spirit and early ecumenicism. Catholic worship now is located in the Church of the Holy Apostles, Winchester Street. Its brickwork and tiling have a sunny Mediterranean air, and a parish hall faces **Cumberland Street**.

The Methodist congregation meets in Westmoreland Terrace, with family "workshops" one day a week for everyone.

HORSEFERRY ROAD keeps alive the memory of the ferry for passengers, horses and coaches which crossed the Thames to Lambeth. One legend declares that it began one turbulent night in the 7th century when St. Peter was taken across to consecrate Westminster Abbey. The ferryman's trade declined after the opening of Westminster Bridge (1750) but the service seems to have continued until Lambeth Bridge was built in 1862.

HUGH STREET. The name Hugh was chosen for the newly born son of the 2nd Marquess of Westminster, and the street recalls his christening in 1825. The passerby should note the ten-panel doors which distinguish the street and parts of **Cambridge Street**. They are the work of Joseph Davis, who put up the houses under Cubitt's overall control.

HUSKISSON'S STATUE. Beside the Thames, in **Pimlico Gardens,** stands a memorial to a man who was described by Peel as "the first statesman of his time". William Huskisson (1770-1830) was President of the Board of Trade and a leader in the campaign to sweep away tariffs, notably the Corn Laws. Such views put him in conflict with much of the Tory Party and after a term as Colonial Secretary (1827-28) he resigned from Cabinet. At the opening of the Liverpool-Manchester railway he was run over and killed by the Rocket. His statue once was situated in the Royal Exchange; today it ponders man's strange mortality in this corner of London, washed by the tides.

JAMES THE LESS. Designed by G.E. Street, creator of the Law Courts, the church of St. James the Less, beside Vauxhall Bridge Road, was reckoned by Eastlake in "A History of the Gothic Revival" as one of the most original and remarkable churches in London. Today its huge, somewhat sinister tower may deter the visitor, but once through the door the truth of Eastlake's words became clear. It is a jewel, a delightful piece of mediaeval mystery.

The church was built in 1859-61 for £5,000 at the request of the Misses Monk, who wished to erect a memorial for their father, the late Bishop of Gloucester. Street, one feels, with this crimson and gold interior gave the ladies much more than they expected. It may be admired on Sundays, immediately before services.

JENNY'S WHIM was the picturesque name of the tavern and gardens which were to be found on the Pimlico side of Ebury Bridge. It was as its height as a place of amusement for the more humble folk during the late 18th century, and was notable for the monsters which leaped at visitors when they stepped on a hidden spring. At that time only a wooden bridge crossed the Chelsea Waterworks and many tipsy patrons are said to have fallen off and drowned. One casualty is thought to have been Nell Gwyn's mother, who lived in the vicinity of the present **Abbot's Estate.** In 1865 the tavern was demolished for the widening of the railway.

JOHN JOHNSON, a stonemason, and his two sons were ahead of Cubitt when it came to developing Pimlico. They began in the Millbank area, near **Horseferry Road,** then moved to the other side of Vauxhall Bridge Road, Here their efforts were restricted by the market gardeners, and at length they foresook Pimlico and concentrated operations in Kensington. Architecturally their work was far from noteworthy, but some endures in Pimlico and on a lesser scale they must be placed among the area's pioneers. Their name is recalled by a street off Lupus Street.

Undimmed, among a flock of restoranti,
the former Churton Tea Room

The founders

At first the land on which Pimlico stands was turned and weeded and cropped by scores of market gardeners, and by other men who tended osier beds across the desolate, often water-logged fields. Highwaymen found a relative haven amid its wastes; small industries set up along the Thames. By the late 18th century, as the Industrial Revolution took hold, London was spreading much too rapidly for the district to be left untouched . . .

THOMAS CUBITT (1788-1855) more than any other physically created the Pimlico we know today. By securing leases over four estates—Grosvenor, the largest, the Crown, the Wise land and the lesser Sloane Stanley tracts he was able to exercise a control that was unique.

Born near Norwich, he had been a journeyman carpenter, then set up workshops in Gray's Inn Road. About 1824, under a lease from the Duke of Bedford, he built houses in Gordon Square, part of Euston Square and other streets, before turning westward. He developed **Belgrave Square**, that glory of Belgravia, **Lowndes Square** and **Chesham Place**, then tackled the Grosvenor land in Pimlico.

Huge amounts of soil were needed to raise the level of the area. Some came from the recently dug St. Katherine's Dock; much of it was dry rubbish. Cubitt did not build every house, but he strongly influenced the methods and designs of lesser contractors. During the 1840s the raising of Pimlico went on at a rapid pace while simultaneously Cubitt engaged in other ventures: Clapham Park, Kemp Town at Brighton and elsewhere. He built the east front of Buckingham Palace, was one of the instigators of **Battersea Park** and helped to bring the Great Exhibition into being. On his death at his country home, Denbies, near Dorking, he left an estate valued at £1 million.

1ST MARQUESS OF WESTMINSTER (1767-1845) succeeded to the Grosvenor lands at a time when London was experiencing unprecedented, not to say hectic, growth. Fashionable society wished to reside in the west, which was where the family possessed large acreage: in Mayfair, Belgravia, Chelsea and the Neathouses (Pimlico).

The Grosvenor Board granted leases, stage by stage, to builders—Seth Smith, Cubitt, John Johnson and others—then in 1825 agreed to Cubitt's grand scheme for Pimlico. Robert, Earl of Westminster, who was created Marquess in 1831, was a considerable patron of the arts and rebuilt the family seat, Eaton Hall, in Cheshire. While acting through the board and its agents he kept a shrewd watch on the London activities, such as the building of the **Grosvenor Canal** (1823). The coming property harvest for the family was clear enough for all to predict but he did not live to see the mightiest of the returns.

That good fortune fell to **Richard, 2nd Marquess** (1795-1869), who took the trouble to interest himself in such things as the form of terrace styling for expanding Pimlico. Before leases were agreed he might require a portico here, a more elaborate window decoration there—many of those features which distinguish the district today. He would, for example, specify granite kerbing where street works were involved. By a twist of fate the second marquess had been born and partly reared in Pimlico. His birthplace was **Millbank House**, near Horseferry Road, which was then one of the family residences, and he attended Westminster School before going to Eton. On his death his estate was valued at £800,000, more than double that of his predecessor.

THE ROYAL GARDENER, Henry Wise (1653-1738), who had charge of the gardens of William III, Queen Anne and George I, has left a legacy of street names in Pimlico, deriving from his purchase of two fields in the district in 1713. **Charlwood Street** is named after his estate in Surrey while **Moreton Street** and **Lillington Estate** recall properties near Tachbrook in Warwickshire.

By the time of his Pimlico acquisitions Wise had achieved fame enough as a master gardener in the French style. Addison described him, and his partner George London, as the "heroic poets" of their calling. In 1709, at the age of 56, he bought the manor of the priory at Warwick where he spent most of his later years.

His descendant, the Rev. Henry Wise, also of Warwickshire, signed an agreement with Cubitt in 1825 for the lease of the Pimlico land, totalling 24 acres, for housing development. Other reminders of the Wise connection exist today in the profusion of Warwicks—the square, mews, way and place.

L

LILLINGTON GARDENS ESTATE takes its name, as did the street which once bisected the area, after one of the properties in Warwickshire owned by the Royal Gardener. The estate was designed by Darbourne and Drake and replaced a close concentration of 19th century housing on the site. Completed in 1973 the gardens include three pubs, an elderly person's home and Pimlico Library. The blending of lawns, apartments and paths is effective; from the point of appearance the project was successful. Longmore Gardens, towards Warwick Way, opened in 1980, does not match its predecessor. The impression is one of ungainly slopes and relentless brickwork.

LITTLE BEN. An anonymous benefactor provided the funds for the restoration of this delightful miniature of the parliamentary clock tower. It had stood at the top of Victoria Street from 1892 until 1964—a reminder of the 19th century love of decorative frivolity which we blank Philistines eschew. It was erected originally by St. George's Vestry and of the £50 provided toward the cost by six private donors a portion came from Watney's, whose Stag brewery was nearby.

LUPUS STREET refers not to the semi-precious stone but to a family name of the Grosvenors, with a Norman connection. Specifically the street honours Hugh Lupus Grosvenor, the infant son of the 2nd Marquess of Westminster, who grew up to become the 1st Duke. At the corner with **Charlwood Street** may be had an unexpected glimpse of the towers of Westminster Abbey. Today it is half-blocked by buildings; in former times it would have been visible across the fields.

M

MARQUIS OF WESTMINSTER public house was named after the 1st marquess, Robert Grosvenor (1767-45). Built during the 1830's it has always had that name and commemorates the elevation in 1831 of the Earl Westminster to his greater honour as marquess. The pub was among the earliest buildings to go up along Warwick Way, a fact evident from the simplicity of the exterior; windows are small and unadorned.

MEWS LOCATIONS. Pimlico possesses one of the most remarkable early Victorian stabling areas in London. Between Warwick and Eccleston Squares a series of them are linked by two tiny streets, namely Warwick Place North and West Warwick Place. For period charm, unmarred by excessive "improvement", the visitor should not miss a walk around this cobbled toyland.

The highlight is **Warwick Mews**, approached beneath a curving vine. A bench welcomes one halfway down the slope from which the rows of miniature residences can be viewed, including London's narrowest green door, once used no doubt by a carriageman and his family.

West Mews, entered through an archway penetrating a terrace block, has undergone residential rebuilding. **Eccleston Mews**, on the opposite side of Warwick Way, contains some business premises but they blend well enough with adjoining houses. The extent of the mews gives a hint of the activity which went on here day by day when the horse-drawn vehicle was supreme.

Belgravia and South Kensington have manicured mews enough, but can they offer curiosities to match cavernous **Dell's Mews**, off Churton Place, whose stable, lately renovated, housed Poore and Sons? Or **Moreton Terrace Mews North**, which seems to tell a tale of nostalgic abandonment, as if the small firms which once operated had closed up at a stroke? Their signs, now fading, can be seen on the archway walls, along with another from the Grosvenor Estate. Who were these people? Where are they now? The green workshop doors, with fretted wooden overhangs, swing open no more at half past seven.

MILLBANK PRISON once stood beside the Thames on the site of the Tate Gallery and adjoining land. It was built in the early years of last century, largely as a staging post from which lawbreakers could be sent to Australia. For many thousands of Londoners this was their last home on blighty soil. The prison had been planned on reforming principles laid down by Jeremy Bentham; rations, for example, were minutely itemised, if on the meagre side.

Transportation to New South Wales came to an end in 1840, and other prisons, such as the "model" Pentonville, were built. Much of the surrounding land in Millbank was taken up for housing and the gaol became surplus to needs. **Millbank Estate** rests upon its foundations.

The name Millbank recalls the 14th century watermill which was part of Westminster Abbey. It was located at the end of what is now Great College Street; at that time the Mill Ditch, a branch of the Tyburn, flowed down to the Thames.

Six blank windows, Churton Street . . . What sense of mystery this early 19th century architectural device can arouse for the passerby. In Pimlico twelve false windows on one wall are not impossible, as at the corner of St. George's Drive and Clarendon Street.

MOZART'S HOUSE. Wolfgang Amadeus was brought to London in 1764, aged eight, to find patronage and broaden his musical experience. His father took lodgings in Soho, but moved for a time during the summer to 180 **Ebury Street**, owned by a doctor. The family remained in London until the following year. During this time Mozart junior wrote two symphonies (K16, K19) and his first vocal composition, God is Our Refuge. A plaque marks the address in Ebury Street.

OUT-OF-THE-WAY PUBS. The Marquess of Westminster was not going to have mean public houses on every corner in his Pimlico. Cubitt had instructions on the point. Thus, amid the respectable sounding Winchester, Alderney and Sutherland streets can be found, at a proper distance, substantial pubs which at certain times can offer a leisurely drink, village style. The Pimlico pub fancier should be sure to visit:

The Greyhound, Hugh Street, which externally is an early Victorian gem, right down to its rows of chimneypots and two lionheads adorning the facade.

Denbigh Arms, in Denbigh Place, the most tucked away of them. Like the others it blends well structurally with adjoining terrace houses. It could be another house but for the brewer sign and, alas, the new black decoration.

The Clarendon, Cambridge Street, retains the scrolled tablet proclaiming its name above the top storey in the best Victorian manner. One clearly to savour.

The Constitution maintains a brisk trade, especially with visitors to London. The facade is pretty, and nothing could be more enjoyable than a glass before the front door on a summer's eve as quietish Churton Street passes by.

OSIERS for the basketweave trade made a useful staple product for the early Pimlico district when willow trees lined its landscape. Willow Walk, now Warwick Way, honoured the link with Salix viminalis. Sadly, only **Willow Place**, jammed with flats and offices, is left to recall an ancient craft.

P

PEABODY AVENUE. For the ultimate in Peabody estates one should go no farther than near Victoria railway bridge. Squat and freckled the residential blocks sit one beside the other—perfect examples of the Victorian reforming streak. How penitential they seem. George Peabody, an American financier, decided to use £½ million of his fortune to help clear the London slums. He would have been able to keep an eye on this Pimlico project since he resided in Eaton Square and died there in 1869.

PIMLICO SCHOOL, huddled in a gulch excavated for terrace basements, must be regarded as the area's most interesting piece of modern design. Opened in 1970 in **Lupus Street** and chiefly the work of John Bancroft it seems all angles and skylights, yet the total effect is pleasing. It provides "comprehensive" schooling for 1,100, with activities for families on Friday evenings.

QUEEN MOTHER CENTRE was opened by the royal lady in 1980, the year of her 80th birthday. The building, in **Vauxhall Bridge Road**, may not be to everyone's taste, but it meets a recreational need for office workers and Pimlico residents. In 1995 the building was extensively remodelled, both inside and out, and new services added for the fitness conscious. The facade, in a kind of smoked glass, was retained, but it is now masked by healthy foliage. More worthy of Elizabeth of Glamis.

R

ROYAL GARDENER public house, now re-named the Slug & Lettuce, is a reminder of the way Cubitt and associates could achieve such harmonious effect on corner sites. The dimensions are never overbearing, the decoration is appropriate - tribute to the builder and an era. The pub, at the junction of Warwick Way and Tachbrook Streets, originally honoured, one imagines, the memory of Henry Wise, who owned fields in the district in the 18th century.

ROYAL HORTICULTURAL HALLS, in Vincent Square and Elverton Street, are interesting examples of changes in taste during the early part of this century. The Old Hall was built to mark the centenary of the founding in 1803 of the Royal Horticultural Society and is suitably elaborate in a not-unpleasing red-brick way. The New Hall followed a quarter of a century later, being opened by Princess Mary in 1928. How the decoration of its predecessor has slipped away. Externally we seem to have more of a cinema—shades of the New Victoria perhaps?

Both halls provide venues for a procession of trade and public exhibitions throughout the year. But their grandest period comes in the autumn with the society's series of floral displays. A visit to one or more would make an excellent prelude to a trip to the RHS's gardens at Wisley, near Guilford, which can be reached by Green Line coach from Eccleston Bridge.

SPREADEAGLE. Long before the pubs of today existed the humble Spreadeagle catered to the market gardeners and wayfarers in lower Pimlico. It was situated near **Lupus Street** but was swept away early last century as the district was converted to smart town houses. **The Gallery**, at Number One Lupus Street, is thought to have been the first of the new style pubs to take its place.

ST. BARNABAS CHURCH. At least one guide-book writer when making a quick run through Pimlico has dismissed Thomas Cundy's works, St. Saviour's and St. Gabriel's, falsely as being uninspiring. What would he think of Cundy's almost simultaneous creation in **Pimlico Road**? Opened in 1850, in what could be called an early English style, its spire climbs to 170 feet, with a peel of 10 bells. In its early days it was something of a ritualistic centre and the scene of hostile demonstrations.

Thomas Cundy (1790-1867) was the son of an architect and builder of the same name who was surveyor to the Grosvenor estate in London. In 1825 Thomas the younger succeeded to the position and held the office for 41 years. He designed many country houses and in later years concentrated on churches in west London; Holy Trinity, Paddington, St. Paul's, Knightsbridge, are among his works. **Cundy Street and Estate** are named after him.

ST. GEORGE'S SQUARE, though open to the public, is sadly the least tended of all the gardens. It was not always so for last century its terraces numbered admirals and diplomats among their residents. The square was begun about 1850, a later and more ambitious project than "the Warwick". On Cubitt's death in 1855 it was still incomplete. Its length and Thames frontage make it notable among London squares. In summer its trees still have the ability to clothe the area in grandeur, while Pimlico Fair in July gives it a jolly community air.

ST. SAVIOUR'S. With a height only 12 feet less than the Monument the spire of St. Saviour's is one of the most exhilarating in this part of London. It needles above the terraces to 190 feet with a clarity unsurpassed. The church was built in 1863-4 for £12,000, the greater part of which was provided by the Marquess of Westminster. It was consecrated nine years after its cousin St. Gabriel's, Warwick Square; both were designed by Thomas Cundy. The little triangular piece of St. George's Square at the church door, framed by tall terraces, forms Pimlico's village within a village. The pavilion-style building in the square is, in fact, an air shaft for the Victoria Line deep below the surface.

STAG BREWERY. A public house named the Stag, at the end of **Allington Street**, recalls the existence nearby of the Stag Brewery, founded in 1660 by Sir William Green, whose family crest included that particular animal. From 1788 the brewery was known as Elliot's and in 1837 Watney's gained possession. It remained a landmark, exuding its breath of malt and hops, until the 1960's when it was demolished for more offices.

SUTHERLAND STREET commemorates the fact that the 2nd Marquess of Westminster chose Elizabeth, youngest daughter of the Duke of Sutherland, to be his bride. They were married on 16th September 1819. **Elizabeth Street** and the bridge over the Southern Region lines are similar reminders of the new Grosvenor connection.

T

TACHBROOK STREET takes its name from the place in Warwickshire, the county in which the Royal Gardener possessed rural estates. But the street might almost be called Bath Crescent, at least at its southern end where St. Saviour's spire rises above the curving terraces. The ideal vantage point is at the corner of **Charlwood Street**; look in either direction and wonder at the sense of style.

One of the area's two street markets operates daily but is most varied on Friday and Saturday. At Number 42, now a newsagent's, was published the first issue of the Westminster & Pimlico Gazette on 18th June, 1887. Before the existence of Tachbrook Street, a branch of the Tyburn followed much the same path before joining the Thames near the present **Tachbrook Estate**.

Porticoes please

The term Italianate-Westminster Portico has been used to describe the architectural style of Pimlico. Yet how Grecian is the spirit of the overall effect upon the eye. Certainly the number of portico columns, and capitals and balustrades, if anyone troubled to tally them, would be staggering enough. One cannot help feeling that the Cubitt workshops, by Grosvenor Canal, must have had half a dozen stonemasons engaged on columns and nothing else, long before Henry Ford thought of dividing labour. Cubitt was the first builder to employ a range of craftesmen full-time, which in turn demanded large scale projects to keep them occupied.

Occasionally the standard column and simple capital give way to the ionic, quite inexplicably, as at the corner of **Alderney** and **Gloucester Streets** and in parts of St. George's Drive. Was it a yearning for change or did a sub-contractor get it wrong? Similarly, as a variation from the garlands and wreaths which grace most windows, some houses facing **Lupus Street** adopt a stylish type of crest.

Curving facades are usually employed at the many triangular street corners, with an often touching period result, and the town layout is designed to create a sense of pleasant vistas and spaciousness. Yet the walker may cover a considerable distance without being aware of the fact or any feeling of fatigue. A gracious urbanity is achieved by clever arrangement rather than massive expenditure.

Peek-a-boo window, at the entrance to Eccleston Mews

TERRACES are at their mightiest in the main thoroughfares, notably Belgrave Road and St. George's Drive. They are particularly impressive where the latter crosses Gloucester Street; here the corner houses mix bulk and style in a very pleasing way. The terrace which straddles that section of St. George's Drive between Gloucester Street and **Denbigh Place** is remarkable for its completeness; every line combines to make the perfect whole—a ducal palace.

The admirer of Stuccoville would do well to begin his tour at this point, concentrating attention on the grid of streets adjoining Lupus Street. As one walks down Gloucester Street almost every corner house delights the eye. The scale of each and their proportions seem sweet indeed, a fact enhanced by tree planting in recent years. Here is the wonderland one seeks. How well the charm is maintained over a wide area.

If the terrace connoisseur wants balconies with delicately curved balustrades of wrought iron he should inspect **Churton Street** (south side) or Tachbrook Street. In Denbigh Place and lower Charlwood Street he will find a distinctive, picturesque type of terracing. **Ponsonby Terrace** on Millbank should not be missed, nor the east side of Vincent Square. But the true buff's heart will soften further when he meets the cosy, loveable mini-houses of **Maunsel Street**, between Vincent Square and Horseferry Road.

TATE GALLERY. The late 19th century was a time of art collectors on a grand scale. It was fashionable and very often mechanical. Few of the rich connoisseurs have had their names kept before the public quite so handsomely as Sir Henry Tate —the result chiefly of his own beneficence and foresight. The sugar magnate wished to present 57 British paintings to the nation but stipulated that they must not become part of the National Gallery or South Kensington museums. In the end he put forward £80,000 for erection of a new gallery while the government provided the land, the site of the Millbank Prison, demolished in 1890. He made possible an extension in 1899 and further benefactions followed from the art dealer Sir Joseph Duveen, who provided a gallery for the Turner collection. Sir Hugh Lane's bequest of modern paintings led to the setting up in 1917 of the Tate collection of contemporary foreign works.

The spirit of private giving continued with the opening in 1979 of new galleries on **John Islip Street** for the programme was financed partly from the Calouste

Gulbenkian Foundation and partly by the government. The extension provided half as much space again as the existing galleries. The Tate contains both the national collection of British art, unique in the country in collecting British works in a systematic way, and the national collection of modern painting and sculpture.

Where does the visitor begin? He or she will want to see the superb Turner works, mysterious Blake and can walk through room after room of contemporary creations, ranging from comic-strip blow-ups in the Pop Art manner to Pablo Picasso, Matisse and thousands of others. There are guided tours, free daily lectures and films. The Tate is at, or near, the top of the London gallery league.

V

VAUXHALL BRIDGE. The present structure was opened in 1906 at a cost of £480,000. The project, mid-stream statues and all, was the work of Sir Alex Binnie. It replaced the original bridge, which was opened as a toll crossing in 1816. The private company set up by Act of Parliament charged a penny for each foot passenger, 2/6 for a coach with six in hand, while cattle could saunter over at sixpence a score. The bridge was declared free of toll in 1879 and the increased traffic soon made its replacement a pressing need.

VICTORIA PALACE. How many would remember the gilded statue of Pavlova which once was poised on the top of theatre tower? It was placed there by Alfred Butt as a tribute to a dancer whom he had introduced to London. It is said Pavlova winced visibly every time she went to Victoria to catch a train. The statue was removed for safety during the Blitz, and has disappeared.

The theatre was designed by the magnificent Matcham, who was responsible for so many playhouses and music halls throughout the country. It was built in 1910 for £12,000 and included a sliding roof for the greater comfort of audiences in warm weather. The Victoria Palace was successor to Moy's Music Hall (1832) and the Royal Standard Music Hall, which opened in 1863. When Butt bought the latter it was the oldest premises in London to hold a music hall licence.

At the start Butt's superb replacement continued the music hall tradition; the opening programme included a one-act play called "The Deputy Sheriff". In the thirties, as difficult times affected the live stage, the theatre adopted the revue craze, though later straight plays were mixed with musicals, until the coming of the Crazy Gang and Flanagan and Allen, who scored enormous success and will always be associated with the Victoria Palace.

VICTORIA SQUARE, which is better described as an enclave, is one of the most endearing pockets of the district and has enviable literary connections. Situated off Buckingham Palace Road, it was a haunt from time to time of Browning, and Thomas Campbell, another poet, lived at Number 8.

Campbell packed up and went to live in Boulogne in 1843 but before departing sold many of his books to any interested parties. His grocer took a liking to a folio volume of sermons because "one leaf of them will wrap a whole pound of raisins".

Two friends of Browning lived in the square, Joseph Arnould, later an Indian judge (at No. 18) and Chorley, who played host at dinner to the great man and other congenial spirits.

VICTORIA STATION was formed in a series of building activities as railways expanded at full steam and then settled down into amalgamation. The iron and glass hemispheres spanning Platforms 1-8 are part of the oldest and most interesting section and included the Brighton Company and the London, Chatham and Dover Railway.

The heavy, yet pleasing, facade looking out toward **Victoria Street** represents the ultimate development into the Southern Railway and was built in 1898. In a bay just inside the entrance can be found an illustrated map of the Southern's routes, preserved behind glass in its period glory. The terminus may not be as spectacular as Brunel's Paddington or St. Pancras but do they have a companion quite like the **Grosvenor Hotel?** Designed by F.T. Knowles it is, according to your taste, an impression in stone of an overweight Kaiser, military hat and all, or a charming recollection of a more leisurely yesteryear.

VICTORIAN NEIGHBOURHOOD SHOPPING. The family bakeries, sweet shops and haberdashers have in most cases disappeared but the picturesque facades remain, though now the occupants may be dentists or travel agents. The 19th century charm lingers, specially in:

Churton Street, whose tranquillity has been restored by the blocking of Tachbrook Street. Its main claim to renown today rests with the Tea Room, which though closed for some years is preserved in all its no-nonsense glory. The former proprietors live on the premises in retirement having served Londoners through many decades. What memories are stirred by the sliding glass panels and the square lettering above proclaiming the "CHURTON TEA ROOM". The visitor might

Worthy of a prince . . . St. George's Drive terrace at Denbigh Place

imagine it was still in business; instead it is a rare memorial to the great age of the London tea house, modest, cheap, dependable.

There were other "cafs" in the street, but all have vanished, along with the British Legion branch and post office on the corner of **Churton Place**. The stroller should make a point of turning into this said "place"—a delightful cul-de-sac, lit by a single gas lamp. Its terraces, along with those of nearby **Charlwood Place** and Churton Street itself would make the ideal early 19th century film set.

Moreton Street can offer even greater peace since, being more isolated, it has suffered most from the move to supermarket shopping. The vistas, white and classical, conjure up Queen Victoria's youthful years, and seemed to be enhanced by the glimpse of the Battersea power station chimneys, which once smoked thoughtfully in the background.

Sussex Street. Ten shops, one empty, and a public house, the Sussex Arms, are gathered face to face at Winchester Street. Who were these shopkeepers of old? What did they offer? Their premises now are filled with a betting shop, hairdresser or estate agent. Healthy young trees, planted by the kerbs in recent years, however, have given new charm to these streets. With St. Gabriel's clock showing five to three it could indeed be a country town of yesterday, of a super elegant kind.

VINCENT SQUARE, covering ten acres, has a sweep and country freshness of its own. It forms the playing fields of Westminster School and is named after Dr. William Vincent, a former Dean of Westminster and master of the school who died in 1815. The land was once part of Tothill ("Tuttle") Fields, and bear gardens were situated there until 1793. In 1810 the area was allocated to its present use; it was enclosed 30 years later. The clubhouse adds to the present village green aspect, which is best enjoyed on Saturdays in summer as the batsmen hit out in centre-field.

WARWICK SQUARE, 140 years on, presents a fine sense of unity and completeness. The terracing is substantial, yet never less than graceful and serene. St. Gabriel's, the gift of the Marquess of Westminster, was consecrated in 1853, and its fine tower and spire almost give the impression of wanting to sail away from the rest of the church. The interior has a mediaeval cosiness about it which is quite appealing.

For one of the loveliest views in central London stand at the Belgrave Road end of the square and see the spire set among the trees—rural England in the great city, as its planners intended. Number 33, the studio of the Victorian portrait painter James Swinton, has been restored by the Warwick Trust as an art gallery and venue for recitals.

WARWICK WAY follows the course of the old Willow Walk, the traditional route across the marshes between Westminster and Chelsea. Today it forms the high street of Pimlico; once it was a narrow, dangerous path with the wayfarer an easy prey to thieves and pranksters. Many poors souls are said to have ended in the ditches on either side. The presence of lines of willows flanking the track has been attributed to Henry Wise, gardener to Queen Anne, though the trees were widespread in the well-watered region over many centuries.

WATERWORKS CHIMNEY. Anyone strolling about Pimlico will, after a while, begin to imagine he or she is being followed by a menacing, brick tower. The effect is most striking from the end of **Clarendon Street**; Victorian industrialism, indeed, declaring itself triumphant. The chimney belonged to the Chelsea Waterworks and was built in 1875, together with the Western Pumping House. The pumphouse, in Grosvenor Road, remains unaltered externally, down to the bowled lamps. To its credit Thames Water has seen fit to floodlight the building and it comes up a treat. A French financier's mansion perhaps? A Belgian bank chamber?

WESTMINSTER CATHEDRAL was designed on a lavish scale late last century and can be considered, at least from its exterior, as an architectural success in a smooth Eastern style. Its founder, Cardinal Vaughan, is honoured in a memorial bay. Alas, the upper reaches of the interior remain unfinished. Those sections which are complete, for instance the side chapels, are stunning in their decorative richness.

Visitors should take the lift (fee charged) to the top of the tower for one of the best views of the area. In a glass case rests St. John Sothworth, dressed in the priestly robes of the 17th century. He ministered to his flock in Westminster until he was captured in 1654 and taken to Tyburn. There he was hung, drawn and quartered.

LOCAL HEROES

Wolfgang   Mozart would have been much amused if someone had prophesised that one day he would stand in effigy near his old summer residence in London. Almost worth a brisk, one-act opera . . . yet in 1994 a statue of him was erected in Orange Square, Pimlico Road,

It honours his stay, with his father and sister, at 180 Ebury Road in 1764, at the age of eight. The work of Philip Jackson, it shows Mozart with a violin raised to his chin and a boyish twinkle in his eyes.

Princess Margaret performed the unveiling ceremony, which was especially fitting since Mozart had played before George III, to everyone's delight.

The house, which survives nearby, was provided for them by a Dr. Randall, and at the time the area was largely open fields. The Strombolo House tea gardens, however, already existed on the south side of Pimlico Road, and the renowned Chelsea Bun House drew many visitors to the vicinity.

● Another maestro, if in bricks and mortar, Thomas Cubitt, received his proper recognition as creator of Pimlico when a statue was put in place at the corner of Denbigh and Lupus Streets and St. George's Drive in May 1995.

William Fawke created a delightful image of the builder standing amid his materials and tools of trade, clearly absorbed in his vision for Pimlico.

The statue was unveiled by the Duke of Westminster, descendant of the 1st marquis, who had agreed to Cubitt's grand scheme on family land.